Poetry which holds l
direction. *Sweet Bo*
choreography of self, desire, and po...
brings you to your knees with the next. Allman is a truly original new voice.
— Olivia Douglass

Esme Allman's début is dancerly, in the sense that dancers give themselves to *this,* but they are not giving themselves to us. On the irreversibility of naming, how being known by your mother is not the same as knowing yourself, on the quest to outrun former versions of ourselves, on shying away from being cast in langour, on self pleasure. I love its ardent sensuality in poems like 'Love Letter'. There is a frenzy in these poems that feel so raw that the sadness hits harder, especially in 'Brat', comfortable in areas of discomfort. *Sweet Bone Girl* is honest in its lens about the specific experience of biracial middle class-hood as separate from minoritized working class communities, and what that separation implies, in poems like 'Little Rich Girl'. Splitting apart the viscosity of celebrity and performance culture as the video vixon 'My Body Won't Retain the Choreography' and 'The Black Pam-Ann'. Straightforward, conflicted, electric, passionate, naughty, and bittersweet work that thinks about technique in poetry with the intentionality of choreo on the page."
— Tice Cin

Esme Allman has written an extraordinary collection — a fearless yet refined exploration of young womanhood, the body, sex, and sexuality, weaving together themes that are as tender as they are ferocious. The mastery of form is especially impressive, with words on the page bending and weaving in a way that mimics the contradictions inherent in the poems' themes. The prose is alive and as full of energy in the way all good poetry is, with the resulting collection holding onto the complexities of joy and grief, dark and light, and strength and fragility, seemingly all at once. *Sweet Bone Girl* is a welcome gift to contemporary poetry and Allman is easily one of the UK's most exciting young poets.
— Bridget Minamore

This collection swells with omnipotence and daring, hollowing out the chest of womanhood and arresting us with limbs, might and a reverence for the sensual. These poems pull us through azure water-scapes, dance choreography, hotels, attics and want, ebbing the parameters of agency, sexuality, fidelity and self-pleasure. Delicious and kinetic, Esme's poems invite us to excavate room in our bodies to plant, feed and prune our desires. *Sweet Bone Girl* is a precious gem.
— Shanay Neusum-James

SWEET BONE GIRL

Esme Allman is a poet, writer and theatre director from South London. Her work explores history, imagined worlds, and desire within the context of black femininity. She has been commissioned to write poems for the Barbican Centre, English Heritage, the Institute of Contemporary Art with BBC Radio 3 and BBC Radio 6, NHS Arts and Heritage, Pace Gallery, and Poetry Vs Colonialism in conjunction with the London Metropolitan Archives. *Sweet Bone Girl* is her debut collection of poetry.

© 2025, Esme Allman. All rights reserved; no part of this book may be reproduced by any means without the publisher's permission.

ISBN: 978-1-916938-82-3

The author has asserted their right to be identified as the author of this Work in accordance with the Copyright, Designs and Patents Act 1988

Cover designed by Aaron Kent

Edited by Andre Bagoo

Typeset by Aaron Kent

Broken Sleep Books Ltd
PO BOX 102
Llandysul
SA44 9BG

CONTENTS

MY BODY WON'T RETAIN THE CHOREOGRAPHY	11
HOLY	14
LITTLE RICH GIRL	16
PREMIERE	17
FEBRUARY POEM	18
SELF-PORTRAIT AS FOXXY CLEOPATRA	19
AMANZA FROM SELLING SUNSET SHARES SOME THOUGHTS	20
SWIM DREAM	22
THE PLAY	23
THE NEIGHBOUR	25
MY MISTRESS	27
THE WOMEN IN TRACKSUITS	28
MY HEART, AN ATTIC	30
WHILST I WAIT FOR HIM TO TEXT ME BACK	32
THE MISTRESS	34
THE BLACK PAM-ANN	35
WHEN IT WAS GOOD	37
MIKE AND I HEAD TO THE BEACH	39
SPECTACLE OF THE OCEAN	41
THE STRANGER WHO BRINGS ME HOME	43
JULIA FOX AS KANYE WEST'S MUSE	45
HE	46
THIS FOR YOUR TENDER WORDS SWALLOWED FOR ONE TWO THREE FOUR FIVE SIX SEVEN— SEVEN MONTHS	47

SICK BED	49
DRIVE DREAM	50
BRAT	52
INDULGENCE DREAM	54
MY MISTRESS	55
HANDS ON YOUR KNEES	56
…& KEN	57
KEN SR.	60
BRUITISH KEN	62
THE MISTRESS	64
GUILT DREAM	65
HIS MISTRESS	67
SPRING CLEAN	68
STUPID DAD	69
LOVE LETTER	70
MUM THE KANGAROO	71
LOVE GROWS HERE	73
2 A.M. ON SHACKLEWELL LANE	75
UNCLE THEODORE	77
BEEKEEPERS	79
NOTES	81
ACKNOWLEDGEMENTS	82

For Gail and Shanay

Sweet Bone Girl

Esme Allman

Broken Sleep Books

MY BODY WON'T RETAIN THE CHOREOGRAPHY

I go again, infinite
body; C-shaped
muscles shifting gear
a ridged landscape forming
momentarily on my back,
before disappearing.
Limbs grow water-
logged, pressurised,
almost combusting.
I persuade arms
to scoop above
my head, a big
inconvenience, my balance
thrown. In everything
I'm trying to feel
less lonely – more
awake. A celebrity moves
onto the street,
casts me in
his latest video.
I watch it
over and over,
told them not to use
my real name.
Esme
is infinity hips, lips
sweat-slicked, pouting.
An arched body.

Marble legs, foot,
the start-end of my crotch.
Could I have an arch
eye? Roll them
the way a body
of rocks might.
I travel as honey
painted abs,
skin as brown
as allowed. Decide
I'm delicious; take a bite
before someone else does.
When I open
my legs they spring
shut; useless. I lay
between them, floppy like
after coming. I wonder
at the prise
in my neck
and if I died
in front of the mirror
what heaven
I might be. A nuisance
bird in the street,
wings sprawled,
its twisted crane
oppositely pushed.
My relevé is too
wide, keep trying
to say pussy. I pop

my arm back,
wrist grinding
my coccyx.
Bone on bone. They say
you're doing it properly
when it hurts
the next day
the one after that
especially the one
after that.

HOLY

I was an acolyte. My cassock hung
just above my ankles, teasing
my scuffed shoes. My wrists
poked out of its white arms.

I hated God, like really
hated Him. Feeling my way
along our dark corridor,
hand out, concealing my drunk,
chewing gum, long after
my curfew. Saturday night
screaming match ensued with mum.
Church was my punishment.

Sunday morning, I turned up
at 9:40, toast crumbs in the corner
of my mouth, butter
on my chin. *Jesus*

mum muttered, ushering me out
the door. I'd light each tealight; created
a freckled glow at his nail-impaled
feet, just to see him smile or
drop his cloth. Either really. And
he would if I squinted enough.

The service was a workout. Mum
kept telling me to hold my light lower.

I was tall, taller than the little old ladies
I served with. Ricky was my favourite.
She had a bracken smile as we took metal
cones to each lit wick at the end of the service,
extinguished the flames and watched
the wax bleed down the gold holders.

Frankincense clung to my hair, swelling
under the steam of my lunchtime shower.

Years later, when I'm playing house
with a man mum reckons I'll marry,
she laughs when I admit to spending
nearly a hundred quid in John Lewis

on candles: two tiny boxes
resting on the table; my credit card
significantly dented. She warns me
about not ruining the candles
by blowing at the wicks. As if

the air gathered in my cheeks
wasn't already holy. Hadn't known

open flames are best smothered.
That it's the elements which fuel fire.

LITTLE RICH GIRL

At fourteen I was already barefoot
in the vineyard out the back
of mum's friend's house. Roamed
the Spanish countryside on a beat-up bike

I'd borrowed from next door. Cycled
to the market donning a sunhat, putting fruits
in a wicker basket. Sun-browned children
sat in my lap, my hushing and lulling linens

dress billowing in the hot breeze and broken
Catalan. I admit it: we were middle class.
It's where I felt most white – singing Beyoncé
pop ballads, rocking in the hammock, sun-stroked

and a bit alone. At sunset, Mum allowed me
just a tipple   of red wine. She preferred I drank
where she could see. And I'd tell
all the boys from school, on a shaky internet line

that dialled up louder than the kids cried
about my summer; my life. All of them aspiring
footballers, smoking bad weed, waiting
for my return to London, where their summer
was a dragging damp Thursday afternoon.

PREMIERE
I knew she was mine all along. I was just waiting for them to find out.
— Cicely Tyson

Is that what knowing looks like? I want to know
Everything. Slip knowing into a gold clutch bag.

Seize knowing with the same ease of her throwing
a pair of white gloves over her forearm.

Forefinger, thumbing the glow on her trophy.
Standing, the rehearsed elegance of knowing.

Somebody old and black recalls it as an inelegant time.
Miles, jazz-eyed, guarding behind a pair of sunglasses.

A room full of sunglasses, their bug-eyed stares.
Half-crescent moon mouth. Left arm in bras bas

accustomed to emptiness, hands naturally crescent.
Neck taut from smiling, grin raising her sternum.

White dress, clinging, neckline down to her sternum.
Is that what knowing looks like? I want to know.

FEBRUARY POEM

I go for a walk. The morning is tight-lipped,
tempting Spring. I'm learning my body

again. A knot of hunger gnaws
a crater into my stomach. I fill it

with want, watching my neighbours enter
and leave their homes. It takes everything

not to greet strangers on the street. How
there are other ways to say I'm lonely.

A red-brick wall is blasted in a shaft
of light. It's rained somewhere far away;

petrichor wafting from the gutters.
I'm surprised by the sureness of my hipbone–

a full and protruding pelvis. There I am,
as I pat the flesh on my abdomen, ignoring

the stinging sensation inside. When I return,
the wake of my morning dishevels the flat.

Abandoned mugs, toast crusts on my plate.
I exhale and there is only sunlight.

SELF-PORTRAIT AS FOXXY CLEOPATRA

Not a halo, nor an orb atop
hovering distant, but an afro–
a mighty large Afro– like a pencil line
drawn around the circumference
of a church top. Canerows criss-crossing
backwards, only stopping at the crown.
Not a lengthy tooth-like jagged stiletto
but a set of roller skates–Quad-skates! –
every move the seductive flow of a broken
kitchen tap. Not a top button in sight
but my tiny frame supporting Boobs Boobs
BOOBS, shoved into a latex bikini
waiting for ample time to burst from my body.
Tenpin bowling Boobs rolling
across the waxed floor. Gleaming,
glistening oil in water, oil on top of water
whispering *Gold Gold Gold.* Not a tongue-in-cheek
pun. Not even a joke. Just a slightly
mistimed punchline, accent groovy
with tainting. Not a voice, just the disjointed
AAVE written by Mike Myers (How on earth
did he get Quincy Jones to cameo–?)

AMANZA FROM SELLING SUNSET SHARES SOME THOUGHTS

I mean sure. I've said some things. Who hasn't?
We're all cave mouthed here. Lips Botox-plump,
straight from a rap video. My lips? No honey,

my daddy's Black. You want to do what to him? Eww. Gross.
What's my secret? I probably shouldn't tell you this but
I keep this white gay guy chained beneath my ribs.

Each morning he rattles at my chest, whining
it's the wrong way round. I threaten to stop my heartbeat.
I need him, his baselessness, his spite because *ohwhatthehell,*

to stay in this game. I start a rumour.
I'm a hoe. You didn't hear it from me. I walk
wavy. Make women hold glares between their teeth

and tongue. The men follow. Is this what it is to be lightening,
to be bleach striking? I'm a mother now. I don't have time
to love my baby off the internet. Hmmm. Right now,

I'm super into acting. I'm playing a character, playing house
with a caricature husband. Everything smells like dead
sunflowers. This is what being a woman is.

Gleaming your own sunset. Runwaying down Sunset, heels
horrid deadly. The sun's shining. I'm back at Starbucks. Not
because I want this, but because of Christine. She needs to feel

entitled; so careless as to hold her laptop and coffee
in the same hand. Christine hovers. *Two weeks after giving birth
I was back doing Pilates. Headstands. It's good for sex.*

We're at a party for Mary's dogs, all of us
wearing deranged veneer smiles, my stub tooth grin sat
somewhere in a Turkish hotel packing her bags for flight.

Someone is thrown in the pool. My blowout kinks
in the L.A. heat. and I cry. I think people know.
Another drink is thrown. I've just had a baby. I don't need

all this drama. Think Louboutin's; Breasts–whatever
comes in pairs. There are no friends here.
Only a black girl you pity
because you don't know if she's black or not.

Until she's no longer ashamed 'til she becomes
that very pity. And all the white girls are just walking BBLs,
acrylic nails and a bad attitude stolen from Paris Hilton
who probably stole that from some poor black girl.

Now we're talking. Actually talking. Literally
talking. Christine's hair is cornrowed, tucks a loose strand
behind her ear. She smiles. It doesn't reach her eyes.
She clears her throat.

*Mary, Mary, Mary, Mary. Mary. Literally. Mary. Mary. Mary.
Mary, Mary, Mary, Mary. Mary.*

Nothing but concrete.

SWIM DREAM

he holds me
the water
what's left of my
body, stiff
resistance as futile
there are so many questions
to ask when
a gush between
wrinkled hands
his tongue
between us
follow me
now bustling
with faceless others
disappearing
in the ceiling
the gaping flesh
swimming costume frills

my limbs beneath
thighs suffocating
weightlessness
understanding

i want
my words become
my teeth
paled peach
caressing the trapped air

he steps from the pool

I call after him
through a plastic hatch

hanging over my pink childhood
lapping in the synthetic currents

THE PLAY
It's the only way to leave, 'I don't love you anymore, goodbye'.
 — *Patrick Marber*

I was cast as Anna
in a university production of Patrick Marber's Closer,
the October after a summer affair.
I brought a black playsuit and a wry smile
to each rehearsal. It screamed
I was keeping it together.

In another adaptation I saw
for the play's 25th year anniversary,
the actress who played Anna was also black; mixed.
Anna, a photographer, the other woman a dancer.
I watched the strip-tease scene with my lips
pursed, thinking that's not how you walk in stilettos,
and my bevel would've weakened knees.

But I was black, without melancholy
tearing my gaze– nowhere near as tragic
as my co-star's. I couldn't have sad eyes.
I had a degree to study for– a world to fix
after all. The director (a man) said I
should wear measured intensity
like expensive sunglasses. I broke the arms
on my Accessorize pair, instead balanced
them on the bridge of my nose whilst fiddling
with the strings on my playsuit.

Mum wouldn't come after I told her
about the white boy I had to kiss

in my first scene. *Come here* he shrugged,
as if a regular occurrence, demanding women
waltz across rooms and kiss him. I wanted to
pound the space between us, thump my loafers
centre stage, before I made the decision
to stand in front of him mouth pouted ajar,
eyes semi-shut; ready.

The night it ran smoothest was when
everyone's girlfriend came. I wanted the audience
to know that I, too, was tragic-could be
beautiful. My playsuit twisted. The legs
of the tripod jammed. The white boy
narrowed his eyes. I stared
vacant above the audiences' heads
into the tech box, hoping
to be sent into blackout. I jumped lines

and the white boy's sneer
broke character. He shook me
by my shoulders and a voice
materialised in my throat.

I was grateful when I came to
by the curtain call. The white boy's eyes swelled
in bed that night. He told me
I was wonderful over
and over. That Anna
was a rockstar-the greatest woman
he'd ever known.

THE NEIGHBOUR

He returns a minute later
floor rattling from the door slam.
A woman's voice - *Fuck!* -
and fucking prefix his name. Sometimes
I call him Mr Fucking. He's my neighbour.
An arsehole. He owns a Tesla.
His trainers are fresh; crisp
white. He has a tattoo on his chest
I start to see in Spring, the ink
peering through the opening
of his crisp white shirt,
fine blond hairs teasing
at his chiselled torso.
He admires a giggling couple
coffee in hand
who admire his car.
He has an umbrella–old
church, a cupola roof
held above his head
to fend him from the rain.
He watches me get wet.
The woman upstairs
is still swearing. He's not married
to the woman he lives with.
She's usually red
wine dress dishevelled hair
soaking her shoulders
wine stains widening

on her wine dress.
The rain falls hard; fast,
and when I turn to look, it's blue sky
poking its tongue out at me.
A little boy drops
a chocolate cake
by the Tesla's front left wheel.
It grows waterlogged.
The curtain jerks
footsteps thump above my head.
My neighbour can't believe it. Leaves
a nasty note through the door. It's
misspelt. The spacing's weird. *That car
is a work o fart! Don't fuck
with me.* When he's with his woman
he beams at me sometimes
leaving a wink in her wake.

MY MISTRESS

Look. I love my wife. She knows nothing
of this. Sometimes I rehearse my sorry
after she catches a whiff of patchouli
radiating from my Adams apple. Or
finds the black lace I keep tucked in my breast pocket.
Hell is the threshold of the Hilton hotel in Waterloo.
Always a pleasant receptionist. My cock nearly explodes
Under the table as my train pulls in. I wince my way
to the front desk, remove my sunglasses,
check-in under an alias: Giacomo Casanova. I mean
you meet me at my best. Whitened, a liar.
You're already bent over when I open the door,
untying your trainers, pulling back your hair. *Stand here*
The space between my feet burns. You plant your face
in my crotch. Everyone still has their clothes on.
I love my wife I keep saying again and again
as you do up my trouser zip. Flushed cheeks,
apologising, I offer you coffee. You accept.
I don't know how to work the espresso machine.

THE WOMEN IN TRACKSUITS

Enter The Woman in the Red Track Suit.
She is yelling into her phone. On the 432 bus
I press my head to the window, oil print forming

on the glass, zigzag pattern from my unruly hair.
I love her passion; it's the same thing
people rate about me, especially the Americans

I've dated. Everything founded
in unfounded confidence.
I love the passion, their Americanness

still charming at that point.
She's the brightest thing
on the street. Her gesticulations

theatre: middle, forefinger and thumb
cocked, aimed at the air, mouth twisting
Dickhead! before the traffic light changes.

My eyes widen, catching her laser
gaze for a moment, before recoiling.
She becomes small, then, just a voice

as the bus pulls away. The oil marked
window blurs. I rub it, hoodie half covering
my hand, stretched over my thumb, index

fingering the window. Enter The Green
Track Suit Woman, new bus stop,
made up like she's trying to be the antithesis

of the Red Woman, though she is
with her lip trembling and worn lipstick,
arguing– probably with a man

like one of my Americans–foolish and steadfast–
'til she can barely speak. I imagine them
both in their own wings of a London theatre,
plastic seats knocking with anticipation, red

and green tracksuits ready to combust
before an audience of wilful onlookers. There is
the tremendous sound of rain.

One American in particular, Daniel (not
his real name) would have liked these women
in theory. All their untethered fury and smeared

make up. That's when you know it's special.
When you argue like you're presenting an egg.

MY HEART, AN ATTIC

The chambranle recently varnished,
I nestle myself into the windowsill.

There are no curtains. What else
is a romantic supposed to do

on the 15th of February? I watch
people avoid the ladder lent up

against the house. This is not about
the house, there in the middle of the city,

in the after sun. The attic carries residuals
of rope – frayed twine from those who chose

to scale their way in. There is no glass.
When the wind blows, it strikes my cheek

hot, whips an idle song into the attic.
The door (because of course my heart

is there at the top, in the attic posing as logic)
had been kicked down by one of the kinder

ones, who let me know they were coming.
Don't dismiss it for a wreckage. I know

where everything is. Allen keys that fit
nothing. Screws; debris. Horizontal light

sunrise, midday, sunset. Nighttime of
cyclicals. Flat nostalgia. Dumb blood and

brain chemistry, sparking outside
the windows– the walls.

WHILST I WAIT FOR HIM TO TEXT ME BACK

I pluck my eyebrows
a brand-new arch. Go window shopping
on Oxford Street, imagining
the woman I'll be
in acid-wash Mom Jeans,
a white crop top,
faux leather waistcoat
when I do the dishes. Nearly book a holiday
to Majorca. Frame a photo
of me and a friend
I've been thinking about
whilst I masturbate. Do some more thinking
about all the men who made passes at
my ex-boyfriend. How he would have text me back.
Time fidgets. I check my phone. Muse on
why I let him call it a pussy. Why
are there bruises on my knee? He's not texting me
because of my bruised knee,
my yellowing teeth, he's fucking his ex-girlfriend.
I just know it. I search
for a set of 24 carat tweezers
online at 3 a.m. Flights
to Majorca. It's when I make my best
decisions; blue glare contracting my pupils.

I take my trip; just me, my pussy
and a pile of books. Laid out on the sand,
I miss church. And Dad (though

not enough to accept his call
beyond filling dead time, the ocean toppling
British kids screaming). At night, my Phone light blasts
through my hotel room, his name flashing
across the screen. I roll over,
fall asleep, wrists crossed over
my head, eyebrows
arched perfect.

THE MISTRESS

Arched back and head pressed into the pillow,
he keeps asking if he's a good person.
I admire my pragmatism. How I can make anything
anything. I say *yes, yes*, that his goodness is more
permanent than heat. That the floor of our Airbnb is
a marital bed. The kitchen counter too. When he's doubtful,
I hook my head around and ask him to look
as he does it, a tear falling from my face.
I have a new name, so I don't get confused.
He comes like an apology. My breath rips and shreds,
sending me out alone into the world.

THE BLACK PAM-ANN

And then there was that time I dated Dennis
Rodman. That's what we called him–

Ruthless, running around Vegas like that.
He'd put it all on Black. We'd throw

our heads back, throaty cackle, let it ricochet
through the casino. My martini glass twinkled

for months. *Baby*, his breathy purr enough
to warm between my satins and silks another long

Vegas night. Basketball? What about it? I wasn't
allowed courtside, clinking my martini glass

filled with blue liquid. I was nasty for Dennis–shaved
my hair matching pink, dusty to deep. Pierced

any available flesh. Prepped my ring-finger
and other such things. We never married.

When we spoke of a family it was living separately;
our own quarters of a Beverly Hills mansion

under constant threat of an imported
black mamba, its skin weeping at our lack

of matrimony. It was *always* Dennis.
We'd be bedridden for weeks at a time. Then

wouldn't speak. Both knowing too much,
unable to unsee, those white sheets

creased raw after a rendezvous,
his mistresses; mine too. Sometimes

when I was running late– I'd arrive
to a bouncy party happening on my hotel bed, and think

about dying. That was before the touching,
the sun unnecessarily red, broaching the curtains

Dennis and I longing to find each other
before dawn (or after dusk, whatever time it was)

amongst the bodies – *Dennis?* I'd call out.
He'd call back, simple, *It's Rodman, baby.*

WHEN IT WAS GOOD

My body an act
of mercy, best
when nauseous,
head on your pillow,
waiting for instruction.
You caught me
at my precipice,
shedding any dumb
confusion. Rummaging
from my crown
to my feet.
An assortment
of assertions; silk
factories in pre-industrial England,
a keen literary eye
for anything from Harlem.
This year I was going to have
an adventure.
Which utterance
could today be?
Fashioned, maybe
from nineties Neo-Soul
or bits I picked off Twitter.
I was microscoped,
pinched between your fingers.
I recall your birthday as one
of two days. Certain of it.
I never knew where

to put my grotesque hands
the length of summer.
Eyes between scaffolding
and sunrise. The gaze itself
clawing its way through
the room. Exposed lip.
Slender arm. Choreographed
madness pattering
on the inside of my skull.
What lack
of knowing –
for you
to decide who I was
at any moment?

MIKE AND I HEAD TO THE BEACH

After all that therapy! And that damn
Jacuzzi in the back of the limo, my exposed neck,

his head immersed in the blue
luminous water. Loud cat eyes

flashing under my lids. We didn't have sex.
We were too sad. Just kinda sat there

naked, nodding intermittently. The driver
lent through the partition, goes 'Where to,

Mr Tyson?' I almost missed the powder
on his nose, he was so pale. 'I'd like to see

the beach' I announced. A car horn sounded
and my breasts bobbed against the jets.

Mike didn't say anything, just sat back.
I straddled him for a bit, but nothing

was worth saying, so I climbed off. New York
was doing its wiggle ripple into day, the sunlight

blazed between buildings, reappeared as we hit
First Ave. My mouth tasted sour. I counted two

cigarettes loose in my bag. We crossed the bridge,
seemed to cross it again. Forty minutes

and we arrived at the beach. The driver sat on the trunk.
Mike walked as he was– butt-naked– out the jacuzzi

and straight into the water. Plonked himself
at its lip, wrinkle-fingered, blood beating beneath
bulges of muscle, harmonising with crashing waves.

SPECTACLE OF THE OCEAN
After Arthur Jafa

Ocean container: rocks   not water–
       its hard matter   a set of cannons

crashing one-after-the-other waves.

The water is molten   bodied   choreographed

inhale and exhale.   Turns the ocean grey

       and at once   the sun is the moon
    looming over the rock-sea.

I dip my arm in.   Watch it wade through   cold light
                                     night light
against the stiff sea.

Our boat tilts, pours back
    into the hot ocean,   we submerge,
                                 resurge
sat with our knees   knocking each other's.
Face-to-face, eyes trained

on the verging
       split pencil-lined day and night.

    The water-rocks climb   the ocean becomes a length.
    Higher, higher. Then,

a tumult   engulfing, chewing. Eventually
    spitting us out
               into its mischievous calm.

At once the moon is the sun.
    Golden hour takes away   the threat of dark.
        I'm thirsty
with sodden clothes   salt
crystallising on my palms and wrists.
We watch the world   twist   on its axis.

A voice nearly mine,
    almost yours,   murmurs between the rocks.

THE STRANGER WHO BRINGS ME HOME

I open my mouth
unveil the night's

soft edges
when I'm on top

o in my face
with one tooth

tiny – a speckled star
thundercloud tongue

lilac almost pink
lapping up the dark

his fingers hook
into dips of my flesh

a bundle of muscles
knotted on my back

his hand threads through
my crooked wig

ladders in my hold ups
pink push-up bra

more wire than lace
universe mouth

my constellation teeth
glittering the whole time

stark morning
dizzies me awake

the sound of plantain sizzling
in the frying pan

JULIA FOX AS KANYE WEST'S MUSE

Legs curled beneath my body heavy glass its serrated edge
lipstick stain in four places cross my arm over my torso and smile
Another? I'm indecisive Someone delivers a new glass brown
liquid pliés before pushing me outside myself he gets louder
ruder all while watching from across the room He's been ranting
for sixteen minutes at this point my eyes glaze over roll back
come back I hold His giant hand between my palms the room
has character then stops feeling less barren Please Baby No More
Parties in L.A. a smirk bursts the banks of our mouths laughter
fleeing I can see why love is complicated here I drag my lip at
its corner down with my middle finger exposing my gum one
bejewelled tooth He mirrors me takes a pair of pliers unhinges the
metal Through The Wire I nod I know the hotel begins to feel like
surrender I shrug off the blazer fold it place it at His feet it costs
more than my rent two months' worth replace the Gucci pumps
step into my Converse say thanks for this evening let His kiss
linger on my cheek never hear from him again

HE

rubs the bridge of his nose. Folds the arms of his glasses. Scrubs callous palms under the cold tap. Calls his mum. Tells her to hand over the phone. Has the same face as the little ones. He stares through the windshield at nothing in particular. Pulls out. Turns the wheel. He practices with his eyes closed; red lips full. Stretches himself out in the garden, let's sideways rain land on his forearms. He's polite to strangers– blinks his eyes and bares his teeth. His pupil dilates, hiding his iris. He dances when he feels good, loose limbed, bent at the knees. He frowns at the sound of sirens ringing around him. He cuts through. He

cuts through. Waves at men sat in the barbershop, whilst jumping the queue. Moistens his bottom lip with his tongue, nostrils flaring. He is an animal looking at me this way, to which he furrows his brow. He tumbles into short fitful sleeps, head tossing amongst the flurry of pillows. He handles me with potent clarity, a vet nursing a wound. He loves like how you should love a beautiful thing who bites. He twitches when he hears a lie. For this he is his father's son: his brother's brother. He labours at the stove, tending to the food like suckling.

THIS FOR YOUR TENDER WORDS SWALLOWED FOR ONE TWO THREE FOUR FIVE SIX SEVEN– SEVEN MONTHS
After Fred Moten

for all our secret ends
sat out in the garden
of your parent's place
chins to the sky
I know, Catford's yours
Blue Borough boy
who else knew
about the mess under the rug
water stains
on the sofa? there were girls
and misunderstanding
you ask me to repeat
what I said we're listening
to A Tribe Called Quest
your brother seems to like me
courtesy *u home?* text
phone light pelleting
the dark I went
a summer sleep deprived
half-eyed conversations
in the mid-morning
sauce splatters above mum's stove
I open myself up
to the possibility
that my business could stay
my business
and despite fury

flowering in a cast-iron pot
we could belong to ourselves again
your voice like a lineage
cleans up on a crumpled
piece of hoodie in Brockwell Park
dry grass blowing in our faces
my legs splotchy; pollen enflamed.
And what about bent-necked
in mum's corridor
camera strapped across your body
shoes parked by the door
scooped up in the twilight–
pre-light–of summer's 3 a.m.
treading back to Catford?

SICK BED
For Aunty Constance

She's not wearing a bra. Her hospital gown droops,
whole body a lopsided smile. Turmeric-stained
fingers giving her figure teeth. The heart monitor steadies,
and she raises her arm in the evening's dim.
Tealight flickering from the bedside table. Four
Get Well Soon cards, a vase of dying
lilies and our shadows make the room sentient. She
keeps readjusting her imaginary cleavage, even
tells me to keep my eyes up. I apologise, sinking
into the bed still warm from her cluster of bones
and her cells, the cells in their multitudes eating
away, not saying anything. Her legs sprawl out, hang
off the end. Her elbow, propped up on the armrest, propping
up her chin cradled in her palm. The nurse brings yet another
pillow and it squashes under her weight. Her face
obscures as she turns to the wall. A foot,
then a calf, last a thigh, launches into the room,
throwing itself over her lap. She holds out
her glass, demanding *Another.*

DRIVE DREAM

I limp from
the wreckage bloodied
body nowhere specific
Frank is already
so far
in front. The trees
are completely
still. They boundary
the empty motorway
a bated breath.
Coughs summoning
themselves where Frank's name
should be.
The back of his head
is a menacing shrink
picking up speed
a deer
plunging from predator
or wolves
toying with their prey.
Feet slapping
the hot tarmac
I run like an accident
and collide
with a door. Clean
vermillion, letterbox
a slit in its face,
golden knocker

a balled fist.
No numbers appear.
The latch clicks
I cross the threshold.

BRAT

I was a dickhead that summer.
Foot stuck out, poised
on the tube rereading the opening sentence
of some award-winning book. Maintained eye contact
with men wearing wedding bands. Stared down
pretty studs in front of their girlfriends like
do you not see this mouth? A woman
at the lido had breasts I wanted– asked her
if she cared to swap as she fumbled
for her towel, searching for her bikini top
that was stashed with my belongings.
Started arguments with my exes, slurring down phone
at 2 a.m.—they owed me money; I wanted my fur coat back;
I was terminally ill. Their annoyance I didn't see
through my bad sexting. I was focused on winning.
Took up smoking after my runs, flipping off
Dulwich parents dragging their bratty kids to school,
my athleisure siren red and skin-tight. Overslept.
Was late to my babysitting gig. Got drunk
after making the kids put themselves to bed.
My parents begged me to see them. Once a month,
on a Sunday I'd flop on their sofa, foul mood
resembling my best friend at sixteen. Boasted
of all the people I cancelled on just to be here.
Took to trying to talk my way into everywhere:
private members clubs; sex parties; sex parties
disguised as private members clubs. Everyone
had to feel as embarrassed as I did. I glowed

pregnant with a greyish void and spewed bollocks
I learned at private school. How to say I've got this
With the same condescension as sucking citrus.
My legs were limitless. Went hiking
to drug dealers' dives in East London. Lured
the most desperate partygoers into the smoking area.
Paraded my grief in a leather harness.
I was obnoxious with my loneliness. Made it
everyone else's problem.

INDULGENCE DREAM

I amass a blubber.
Layer of fat
between my skins
shielding against
tough Antarctic
blowing its ice wind.

In another scene, I'm mud-
trodden, sludge bellied
and eating until my cheeks
bloat, beyond sated.

And this is just my body. Sometimes
my hands fatten, cashmere
gloves in a Chicago winter.
My clothes always get bigger

and bigger. Here's where I feed.
Dining room table,
a Juliet balcony–maybe
a cigarette drooping from my lip.

I gorge at the itch I have become
and my appetite subsides.
This wanting gnaws
with its wanting teeth.

MY MISTRESS
After Chet'la Sebree

I love my wife. She knows nothing of you.
Purgatory is a Premier Inn
off Birmingham New St. I remove my sunglasses,
check in under a fake name: Tiger Woods.
You meet me at my best; whitened,
a liar. You fist raps on the door
and I go a little soft. On the floor your limbs sprawl.
'Lay here,' I say patting the bed.
You crawl into my lap. I remember the cat
hasn't been fed. Your pupils dilate. *I love my wife*
I say again and again as you work
to undo my shirt buttons. Bare-chested,
I offer you coffee. You decline. There's
grit in my eyes. I fold my pyjamas.

HANDS ON YOUR KNEES

I watched him put his hand on my knee. He watched
as he put his hand on my knee. His hand eyed
my knee, then grew closer. My knee
scarcely moved as he lay his hand on my skin.
His clammy fingers thrummed at the point
before the material of my dress started. My shin, tucked
behind my calf, writhed under the table.
His shoe swiped the inside of my calf. I heard
the crack in my neck as he spoke. He put his hand on my knee.
He placed his hand on my leg. He put his skin
on mine. Flesh to flesh. He turned me
into a body. He cracked me open
with his eye. My knees refused instruction.
I pretended not to notice.

I pretend not to notice. Fold my hands
in my lap. He has his hand on my knee. I can't
keep count of how many hands there are.
I blink my thighs shut, slit with sleep. They doze
closed. He notices. I notice him notice. Again, I pretend
not to notice. His noticing is a rabid dog, a shark's
gaping mouth, a hissing cat clambering about
my lap. He puts his hand on my knee, and I count
how long it is until I can leave. Time is a breath.
I guzzle the air. Long and slow between my cheeks.
I take an inhale. Sip my drink. Hand
at the base of my thigh. Dress hitched. He watches the hem
rest on my knee. Tugs. Replaces it
with his lecherous hand.

...& KEN

one

I have met white men
bouffant hair
gelled quiffs lips
an incision. A command
instead of a voice:
ComeIn SitDown
LookAtMeWhenI'mTalkingToYou

two

His signet ring
started telling
the wrong people.
Hands bleached
in the absence
of hard labour.

three

Ken works in luxury
Nightclubs. As an estate agent. In
finance. Ken (legally Kenneth
Junior) is dating
at the moment. His alcohol imbued
zig-zag out the bar. Hails
a cab, whilst his date, pretty,
blonde, smarter than this,
looks to the sky

four

where sex with Ken is
on the other side.
Her heart stirs.
I've just gotta make it to morning.

five

I'm a cocktail waitress. An adult
babysitter Watched Ken play
with his dolls in booths,
on high stools, at tables
by the door. He sends me a look
at the end of his dates: when will I stop
messing around?

six

A long black
and Chanel Bleu
wipes him clean
from his hangover.
Rolls over. Texts his friends.
He loves them–known them
since school since
college since

forever. Tells them
about the pretty blonde.
How she reminds him

of his mom. Ken's parents
died a long time ago in the South.
Moved to Providence
as Barb and Ken, reeking
of new money.

seven

Ken cries as he cums
his trust fund doesn't release
for another eight months   not
that he's been counting

eight

Ken sometimes goes
to the bad part
of town. Parks a mile away
and walks. Keeps bugging
me at the bar. Tips me.
Wants to know
if he can call it
a pussy. This is all practised

nine

in the mirror. I watch
through the bangs
of my blonde wig
gaps in the synthetic hair
cracks in a door

KEN SR.

I practise in the mirror
like my ancestors did.

I'm southern blooded.
My wife too. Ain't she

a belle? We worked her
accent out her throat.

Replaced it with
the monotonous croak

of Long Island and
suburbia and casual

racism. I know honey,
just a couple more hours

until we reach
the Hamptons. She's

a good wife. Don't
snub her. We worked

for this. Barb hands me a pair
of loafers. Tuscan leather.

Reassures me I'm
her favourite out of all of us

(including the kids). I'm
an only child. My Dad had

others, a second family.
We used to do Christmas

together. As a kid, he told me
to hit the sidewalk, the street.

*You gotta sell Kenny – these people'll
buy anything.* My half-siblings

recall, from the spoils
of their childhood, him

bargaining the same way.
I hoist my son in my arms,

get him to look
in the mirror Repeat

after me: *I'm the bullshit
detector. An animal.*

Don't fuck with me.
The boy babbles

in my arms. Barb
takes him off me.

BRUITISH KEN

I keep getting
more beautiful
with age. My eyes darken,
the pupils dilated,
darting between blood vessels.
This growing voice in my throat
like *Come In Sit Down*
LookAtMeWhenI'mTalkingToYou.
Can I be honest a sec–?
Everyone wants to sleep with me
in pub cubicles
just to get thrown out.
Beer froth on my cupid's bow;
knickers round her ankles
court shoes clipping the tiles.
I know I'm being
a gentleman
doing dad proud
when her mascara's still intact.
You're seeing each other
again? A text from her friend lights up
on my bedside table.
It's special this time
I reassure her–I'm not throwing away
the eggshells. Moon shine climbs
up the kitchen wall. I
take myself to bed at 3 p.m.,
twisting the sheets, fever dreams

taking me back to my childhood
lying face down, trying
to suffocate the pillow. I wake
sat on the toilet, closed lid
sending a shock from my
groin to my neck. I could break
into theatrical sobs–
wear her mascara
just to smudge it– tears
tickling my cheek.
I keep saying
I'm an animal
I practise
in the mirror.

THE MISTRESS

That man showed me his teeth so
I don't pronounce his name properly.
It's okay. I'll only need it when I come.
By then it will be two less vowels. The tendons
in my arms a clutter of stuttered constants, vein ridden.
Tense and flex. Fires in the winter are harder
to look away from and I didn't plan on being miserable or
meeting his wife. On the threshold of my Airbnb
he pulls up his T-shirt, shows me his stomach flesh,
and a half-waxed chest. Claims to have an appendix scar
he wants my mouth to explore, although the skin
is smooth, dark hairs whirlpooling at his nipples.
I'm not drunk. I promise. Before we part ways,
I ask him to hold the soft part
of my neck and remind me
how to say his name.

GUILT DREAM

Our hotel balcony overlooks a lake
From the 5th floor. A jetty protrudes
into the murky waters below. The hotel
sells summertime. Out back its
pissing down. We're sat on the jetty, fishing,
legs dangled over rickety wood, raincoats
fastened up to our necks. We use wood blocks,
long cuboid rods, that will freshwater
animals onto its flat surface, before
gently lifting them out of the lake.
I grow impatient. Start
to bludgeon. Club
the foggy water
until it reddens. I look
to see if anyone saw.
I am alone in the rain.
It swells the lake – the water
rises quick quick. I scramble
up the jetty, blood at my heels,
frantic water splashing – its carnivorous
rage. My teeth catch
my tongue as I bolt

for the hotel room on the 5th floor. Calm
chatter unravels between the three of them.
Their bodies lolling on the bed, speaking
a different language. The blood
an inconvenience to their languid gibberish.

I try to apologise to one– another woman. Can't find
The words. Instead fill her suitcase
with the lake water now pooling in our hotel room
bloating the carpet. Ruining the fun.
Its sloshy scarlet drowns her belongings.
I place a handwritten note, delicate,
in the top, explaining myself, my sorry
scrawled under my name. The writing
child's etchings. She tells me to use my mouth
and I grow in the village idiot. 'Get dressed.
We're going to a wedding! You're my guests'.
We're all thankful to leave the hotel room.

At the wedding I abandon the three of them
as soon as there are enough people. Keep them
in my periphery. Promise another drink, a dance,
another time. The waiter presents my food:
an uncooked fish, swimming
in its innards. A delicate note on top.
I blotch the blood on my face
with a wet napkin.

HIS MISTRESS

I meet her because I want to meet shame,
unabashed and flaunting. At least she does not graze my leg
under the table. That's reserved for my husband.
He is a dog. I admire his taste– she, a sweet bone
tucked into a halter-neck dress. It's funny
what allures us. I want to imagine out of the sun she is dead
light, glowless. It's the laughter though, I can hear it now
in the steady conversation. She flinches
at his touch, the same way you would welcome it.
I've seen something I wasn't supposed to.
Replace my sunglasses on my face,
light a cigarette I don't smoke.

SPRING CLEAN

This attic can be accessed by a flight of stairs. Each weave upwards in different twists and shapes. They all lead to the same place. I'm still sat in the attic. A whole day can reverse a wreckage. The ladders have gone. The rope too. The glass is intact although the dust doesn't dance. In shafts of light the sun comes in blinks, and I smell like oud and zinc. Say aloud I am rock; I belong to the land. Like a promise to return. A leather curiosity shrouds me, and my limbs are long enough to run.

STUPID DAD

giving me my inheritance in
an Athletics Competition. Second podium
stick legs staked in my running shoes.
Four hundred metre. Sports bra
plastering my chest to my chest.
I was quick (trust) and Chloe
was a liar. Standing top podium, plastic gold
medal decorating her decolletage. My teeth
snapped together in a tight grin for the photo.
The diligent whisper of my classmates
that she had cheated, sped up and down
the coach on the way back to school.
My plum knees knocked on the seat in front,
further bruising me. Petulant head hung. Boobs
still small. Face like dad's. Legs
like dad's plummeting the pavement
disembarking the coach. Even when I raced–
limbs like his cigarettes ashing
on the tarmac, a little dust in my wake
as I approached the finish line.

LOVE LETTER
After Lynette Yiadom Boakye's Citrine by the Ounce

Black men get beautiful like that, blooming
in autumn when no one's watching. Tangled
eyelashes from fistfuls of sleep. Beard plumage;
a hand-grabbed bouquet. Nappy-headed.
Halo-faced. He lights the kitchen to daybreak,
and the sun haemorrhages at the glass. His chin cleft valleys.
And with a voice that climbs up the flat of his nose.
Coffee granules lodged under his nails. Adam's apple
rolling up his neck, loosening at his collar,
clerical-like, hairs sprouting at the open buttons. I wait for him
to blink up at me and reveal two hazel-green
brown-black eyes. Feline; with bite. Instead,
stems of dark rum crawl along the inside of my glass.
A sharp exhale darting through pursed lips. He doesn't flinch.

MUM THE KANGAROO
After Ocean Vuong

She's there when I arrive. Bach's Cello Suite
No.1 in G-Major ends. She tells me to wait
for the solo. Like most lonesome kangaroos,

she bounces on the spot as the waiter takes
our order. Warns her to stay in her seat,
stumbling over 'madam', the word trapped

in his clenched jaw. Our starters come.
My soup lands hot metal on my tongue. Mum,
the kangaroo, boasts she sat us in the window

specially. Everyone has a look. The restaurant
came recommended from a friend of hers
I've never liked– who would recommend

a restaurant, with little space for a Kangaroo
and her daughter. In other words
she's a bitch. The wait staff are charming

in the way you're paid to be.
I order the most expensive thing
I can afford. I want them to like me.

They bring me tap water and Mum
makes to punch the left slice
of my high cheekbone. *Stop thinking*

about your Dad. I'm not. Really. It's
just the chef. He thinks it's my birthday.
She peels the loose skin at her pouch.

Structural inversions: bone, fur, skin pulled
pale, greying. *See, I'm never alone* she pats
and her pocket gives a soft shut

of a sash window, not before I catch
a peek of the little kangaroo nestled

between her inner and outer body.
I wonder why I am not a Kangaroo.

LOVE GROWS HERE
For Mum

There's a baby   a perpetual protruding
     stomach swoll the skin   grafting itself

     at my belly button
         down   to my pubis.

     I wear white– well   not quite white,
     Champagne   beige   off-white

     a dress with the middle   cut out   so
     baby can poke   through. My areolas visible

     the linen   the lot
     there is no beating

     on the inside of myself– ourselves–
     she sleeps   whilst my skin   stretches

smooths   is   sunkissed despite the winter
     in this hold we   are double-lifed

     adulted, child-like. I plunge
     my hand in water. She likes the tapping

     of rain on downstairs' roof though she
     recoils from the ocean and so I pass

on the epidural. Too much

    expanse for something so small. She's breech.

After all that pushing,
    they caesarean their way in. Twenty-two minutes

    and she materialises: a cocoon
      the world has not yet touched. Neither of us cries.

2 A.M. ON SHACKLEWELL LANE
After Warsan Shire

Looking towards home, eyes bright, clothes
ash-soaked, bare arms gathered outside
a pub, my head in your lap, your hand
on my back, walking too long, too drunk,
East London: a big small.
Traffic lights blinking a milky scar tissue eye,
everyone else moving in reverse.
There is ecstasy in repetition.
I slide a plastic tenner across the countertop.
You thank me with a squeeze.
Greasy finger suckle and laugh, I say
'I love you' skimming chicken bones
into the curb like stones.

Like stones skimming
a chicken bone curb I say, 'I love you'.
Greasy finger suckle and laugh,
you thank me with a squeeze I slide.
A plastic tenner across the countertop.
The ecstasy of repetition moving
in reverse. Everyone else a milky scar tissue
eye. Traffic light blinking a big small.
East London too drunk. Walking too.
Long your hand
on my back. My head
in your lap gathered outside.
A pub

bare arms
ash-soaked clothes
eyes bright. Looking
towards home.

UNCLE THEODORE

I have an uncle. Soft-spoken.
Star Wars fan. Can be found

laser focused, crooning
the *ggzz* sound of his light saber.

I didn't see him for years. Dad told me
he'd gone missing, though to where

he wouldn't say. He likes the moon
and the planets. If he could, he'd go.

That started the rumour about him
coming to the door in a babydoll.

Blue negligée. A flitting giggle
identifiable by only the women

in my family. Once, on the way
to Grandma's, I bumped into him

on her road. Cowed against licks of wind
I slackened, squinting for her worn

cerulean door. Thought before I knew
I was sure – that's Uncle Theo. He didn't

register me. *Uncle Theo,* I called.
Startle, then recognition, his face bursting

into doughy joy. He said I looked wonderful
like I should be reporting on the news.

BEEKEEPERS

Our car breaks down somewhere in the French
countryside. Sap pools on the trunk
of a Cypress tree, stretching up to the sky. We mount
the hard shoulder. I hold you– against
the caprices of foreign radio– hot
in my mouth, pincer words in your teeth.
We make love in every city. Masses
of tourists gather on cathedral steps
where you catch my hand behind my turned back.
The days scorch, sun burning our noses, skin
flaking on our shoulders. We cross the Italian
border; argue over my mispronunciation, my
caricaturing. You in an angry, low voice, 'It's apé,
amore'. The same marred inflection on each end.

NOTES

1. 'Premiere' was originally commissioned by Barbican Creative Learning for their *Subject to Change: New Horizons* presented online July 2020 to July 2021, and as an installation at the Barbican Centre in July 2021.
2. The series of 'Mistress' poems were written in response to Chet'la Sebree's beautiful and arresting collection by the same name, published in 2019.
3. Spectacle of the Ocean was written in response to Arthur Jafa's AGHDRA that was exhibited as part of his exhibition MAGNUM at The Louisiana Museum of Modern Art in Humlebaek, Denmark, October 2021.
4. 'This for your tender words...' was written after Fred Moten's poem 'arthur jafa and greg tate' published in his collection *B. Jenkins* in 2010.
5. Love Letter was written after Lynette Yiadom Boakye's painting 'Citrine by the Ounce' (oil on canvas, 2014).
6. 'Mum the Kangaroo' was written after Ocean Vuong's The Bull from his collection *Night Sky with Exit Wounds*, published 2016.
7. '2 a.m. on Shacklewell Lane' was written after Warsan Shire's 'Backwards' published in 2014.
8. 'Uncle Theodore' was first published in the anthology *Articulations for Keeping the Light In*, by Flipped Eye in July 2022.

ACKNOWLEDGEMENTS

To Aaron Kent, for welcoming me to broken sleep with such excitement for and interest in my work. And to Andre Bagoo. Thank you for your close eye and generous editing of these poems.

To Bridget Minamore, Cecilia Knapp, Jacob Sam-La Rose and Rachel Long, for your guidance and tutorship.

To the Poetry School, their tutors and fellow participants, thank you for your suggestions and questions; for meeting my work earnestly and kindly.

To Jack Priedeux, Dom Ansell and Reena Kalsi, for all your support during my creative residency at the Roundhouse. Many of these poems are from Delectably Red; it was a joy to develop my practice with you.

To past and present Barbican Young Poets' and Roundhouse Poetry Collective cohort, particularly Antonia, Jeremiah, Tice, Gboyega, Lola, Maeve, Annie, Sumia, Kareem, Simran, Kerrica, Olivia, Troy, PJ and Kobi.

To Seren Adams, thank you for championing my work.

To those who afforded permission, particularly Savannah Steyn, Alex Evans, Bekah Williams.

To Aaron, Benin, Elete and Isabelle. Thank you for your unwavering support and endless creativity.

To Azzam Merchant. I am grateful for your eye. And your infectious laughter.

My grandmother, who is a spectacular storyteller and who has made me laugh until my face streamed with tears. To my abundant family.

To my father, Colin. Your wit, your agitation and your labelling of me 'yuh see yuh– militant!'. Your love for me is apparent and so very, very felt.

To my mother, Susan. Your encouragement is unparalleled. You resourced my creativity beyond your means. We are always indebted to our parents, but to you, I strive to honour you (with no lilies, I promise).

Safi. After all these years, you have been nothing short of brilliant.

Elijah, this collection existed as fragments across folders and files before your igniting. Thank you for your love and vitality. Your belief in me is palpable.

Shanay, what a privilege to have found you in this life. These poems sit in conversation with yours. I am excited for the poets and women we grow into every day.

Dearest Gail. Everyone deserves a friend like you. I am privileged to know and love you. You inspire courage and light, which these poems endeavour to embody.

LAY OUT YOUR UNREST